Laughter
FROM THE
Pearly
Gates

BOB PHILLIPS
CARTOONS BY JONNY HAWKINS

HARVEST HOUSE PUBLISHERS
EUGENE, OREGON

Cover by Terry Dugan Design, Minneapolis, Minnesota

LAUGHTER FROM THE PEARLY GATES
Copyright © 2004 by Bob Phillips & Jonny Hawkins
Published by Harvest House Publishers
Eugene, Oregon 97402

ISBN 0-7369-1462-5

**And in one quick turn,
Lot's wife became a pillar of her community.**

Abraham

Question: What were Abraham's words to Lot when he chose the better land?

Answer: Thanks a Lot!

Adam and Eve

Adam was the first man to know the meaning of rib roast.

☺ ☺ ☺

Adam was rejected for Eden the Apple.

☺ ☺ ☺

Question: What did Adam and Eve call their first anniversary?

Answer: New Eve's Year.

☺ ☺ ☺

©2000 Jonny Hawkins

Splitting the first Adam gave us Eve, a force which ingenious men through the ages have never gotten under control.

ᘓ ᘓ ᘓ

Eve was nigh Adam; Adam was naïve.

ᘓ ᘓ ᘓ

You'd have a net prophet

©2001 Jonny Hawkins

Conversation between Adam and Eve must have been difficult at times. They didn't have anybody else to talk about!

⑥ ⑥ ⑥

Eve was the first person to eat herself out of house and home.

⑥ ⑥ ⑥

Adam and Eve were the first bookkeepers. They invented the loose-leaf system.

◎   ◎   ◎

Whatever other problems Adam may have faced, he at least never had to listen to Eve complain about the other women who had nicer clothes than she had.

◎   ◎   ◎

When Eve tried to get out of the garden without him, Adam called to the Commanding Officer, "Eve is absent without leaf!"

◎   ◎   ◎

Question: At what season did Eve eat the fruit?
Answer: Early in the fall.

◎   ◎   ◎

Adam speaking to Eve: "Listen, now! I wear the plants in this family."

◎   ◎   ◎

"You hurled an insult, then an accusation...
now I'm gonna start the mudslinging."

©2002 Jonny Hawkins

Eve blamed the snake. And it's true. The snake didn't
have a leg to stand on.

❀ ❀ ❀

You might say that creating Eve was the first splitting
of the Adam.

❀ ❀ ❀

Adam: God, why did you make Eve's skin so soft and nice to touch?

God: So you would like her.

Adam: But what I really would like to know is: Why did you make her so gullible?

God: So she would like you.

Angels

A conscientious minister decided to get acquainted with a new family in his congregation and called on them one spring evening. After his knock on the door, a lilting voice from within called out, "Is that you, angel?"

"No," replied the minister, "but I'm from the same department."

⑥ ⑥ ⑥

A girl whose father was a photographer was out fishing with her parents one afternoon. Suddenly, a storm came up, and there was a brilliant flash of lightning. "Look," she said. "The angels are taking pictures of us!"

Ark

Ark: An injunction to listen, as in "Ark, I think it's raining!"

"All day every day it's pyramids, pyramids, pyramids...
oh well, it beats a cubicle."

©2001 Jonny Hawkins

Atheist

Pity the poor atheist who feels grateful but has no one
    to thank.

☺ ☺ ☺

The atheist can't find God for the same reason that a
    thief can't find a policeman.

☺ ☺ ☺

John the Baptist visits his favorite fast-food restaurant.

A little boy once considered becoming an atheist, but gave up the idea. They have fewer holidays.

Image **is** everything...the image of Christ

©2001 Jonny Hawkins

An atheist is a man who looks through a telescope and tries to explain all that he can't see.

◎ ◎ ◎

Three atheists were trying to bother a young Baptist minister.

"I think I will move to Nevada," said the first atheist. "Only 25 percent of the people are Baptists."

"I think I would rather live in Colorado," said the second man. "Only 10 percent of the people are Baptists."

"Better yet," said the third atheist, "is New Mexico... only 5 percent there are Baptists."

"I think the best place for you all is Hades," said the minister. "There are no Baptists there!"

◎ ◎ ◎

Atheist: Do you honestly believe that Jonah spent three days and nights in the belly of a whale?

Preacher: I don't know, but when I get to heaven, I'll ask him.

Atheist: But suppose he isn't in heaven?

Preacher: Then you ask him!

◎ ◎ ◎

A pastor was speaking when he noticed that an atheist in the audience got up and started to walk out. He was a man who had given the pastor a very hard time.

"Don't go just now," he pleaded, "I have a few more pearls to cast."

Attendance

"Does your husband attend church regularly?"

"Oh, yes. He hasn't missed an Easter Sunday since we were married."

B

~ ~ ~

Balaam

"I'm thankful that the Lord has opened my mouth to preach without any learning," said an illiterate preacher.

"A similar event took place in Balaam's time," replied a gentleman.

Baptism

I don't mind going to a church service in a drive-in theater. But when they hold the baptisms in a car wash, that's going too far!

⊚　⊚　⊚

An Episcopalian minister was about to baptize a baby. Turning to the father, he inquired, "His name, please?"

"William Patrick Arthur Timothy Owen Tyler John MacArthur."

The minister turned to his assistant and said, "A little more water, please."

"I have to do public speaking?
Ugh! Now I have heartburn!"

©2001 Jonny Hawkins

Baseball

Baseball is talked about a great deal in the Bible: In the big inning, Eve stole first. Adam stole second. Gideon rattled the pitchers. Goliath was put out by David. And the prodigal son made a home run.

Belief

It is always safe to follow the religious belief that our mothers taught us; there never was a mother yet who taught her child to be an infidel.

—Josh Billings

Believe

Joe: Say, what do you believe about God?

Moe: I believe what my church believes.

Joe: What does your church believe?

Moe: My church believes what I believe.

Joe: What do you and your church believe?

Moe: We both believe the same thing.

Bible

Dust on your Bible is not evidence that it is a dry book.

@   @   @

A Bible stored in the mind is worth a dozen stored in the bottom of one's trunk.

—Robert Harvey

@   @   @

One of the best evidences of the inspiration and infallibility of the Bible is that it has survived the fanaticism of its friends.

@   @   @

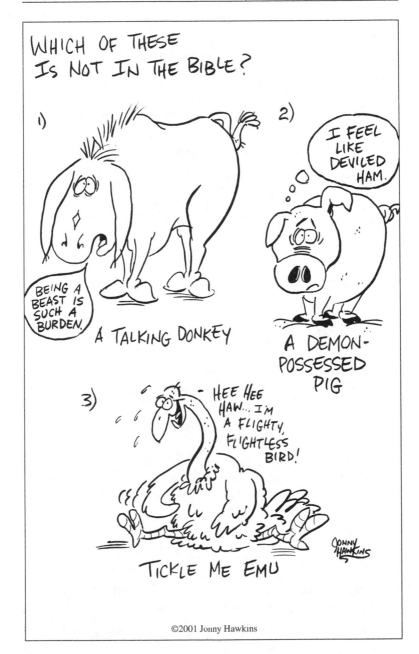

If all the neglected Bibles in this country were dusted off at the same time, we would suffer the worst dust storm we have experienced in many years.

@ @ @

The reason people are down on the Bible is because they're not up on the Bible.

—William Ward Ayer

"My Lord, my Creator, my Primary Caregiver..."

©2001 Jonny Hawkins

Bigots

There are two kinds of people in your church: those who agree with you and the bigots.

Boat

Did you hear about the pastor who bought an old used boat? He named it Holy Scow.

"And so I buried my treasure here...where it is safe."

©2001 Jonny Hawkins

Bowling

Did you hear the one about the ministers who formed a bowling team? They called themselves the Holy Rollers.

Bulletin Announcement Goofs

- Don't let worry kill you—let the church help.
- Thursday night—Potluck supper. Prayer and medication to follow.

"Well, here—let's play catch with this unleavened Frisbee."

©2002 Jonny Hawkins

- Remember in prayer the many who are sick of our church and community.
- For those of you who have children and don't know it...we have a nursery downstairs.
- The rosebud on the altar this morning is to announce the birth of Rodney Allen Carlson, the sin of Rev. and Mrs. Carlson.
- This being Easter Sunday, we will ask Mrs. Burnham to come forward and lay an egg on the altar.

- A bean supper will be held on Tuesday evening in the church hall. Music will follow.

- The organist invites any members of the congregation who enjoy sinning to volunteer for the choir.

- Ladies are requested not to have children in the church kitchen. They make too much of a mess.

- Our pastor will preach his farewell message. Afterward, the choir will sing "Break Forth With Joy."

- Rev. Williams spoke briefly, much to the delight of his audience.

- The eighth-grade students will be presenting Shakespeare's "Hamlet" in the church basement on Friday. Everyone in the congregation is invited to attend this tragedy.

- If you don't like what you hear on a given Sunday, your sins will be cheerfully refunded.

- Due to the pastor's illness, Wednesday's healing services will be discontinued until further notice.

- There is joy in heaven over one singer who repents.

- The youth choirs have been disbanded for the summer with thanks of the entire congregation.

- Please bring your baked goofs for the Fall Sale.

WHAT DOES JESUS SAY IN MATTHEW 5:9 ?

1) BLESSED ARE THE PIZZA MAKERS

2) BLESSED ARE THE PACEMAKERS

3) BLESSED ARE THE PEACE MAKERS

"God said to <u>not</u> eat from the Tree of Knowledge? But I thought He said to be fruitful!"

- Our missionary speaker is Bertha Blech from Africa. Come tonight and hear Bertha Belch all the way from Africa.

Burnt Offerings

Teacher: In our lesson today we have talked about the burnt offerings offered in the Old Testament. Why don't we have burnt offerings today?

Student: On account of air pollution.

"That seems so sack religious!"

C

Cain

Heckler: Who was Cain's wife?

Preacher: That's a good question, but if I were you, I wouldn't be too concerned about other men's wives.

Cannibals

Then there's the missionary the cannibals couldn't boil. He was a friar.

⊚ ⊚ ⊚

Sunday school teacher: What message should missionaries teach the cannibals?

Student in class: To be vegetarians.

Children

Letters to God from Little Children

Dear God,

Did you mean for giraffes to look like that or was it an accident?

—Sally

The Prodigal Son's father has a bad heir day.

©2001 Jonny Hawkins

Dear God,

Why did they talk so funny in Bible times?

—Norman

Dear God,

Please send Willard Anderson to a different summer camp this summer.

—Angela

"Indeed, the very hairs on your head are numbered,
which—with you two—is very interesting..."

Dear God,

Maybe Cain and Abel would not kill each other so much if they each had their own rooms. It works out okay with me and my brother.

—Carl

Dear God,

I keep waiting for spring, but it never did come yet. How come? Did you forget?

—Jon-Mark

Christian

There is one single fact which we may oppose to all the wit and argument of infidelity, namely, that no man ever repented of being a Christian on his death bed.

—Hannah Moore

Three Kinds of Christians...

1. Rowboat Christians have to be pushed wherever they go.

2. Sailboat Christians always go with the wind.

3. Steamboat Christians make up their mind where they ought to go, and go there regardless of wind or weather.

"I beseech thee, O sluggard, to ooze it or lose it...
because I am the salt of the earth."

©2002 Jonny Hawkins

Going to church doesn't make you a Christian any more than going to a garage makes you an automobile.

—Billy Sunday

Christianity

Christianity is bread for daily use, not cake for special occasions.

ⓢ ⓢ ⓢ

Christianity has not been tried and found wanting; it has been found difficult and not tried.

—G.K. Chesterton

**Variations in 2 Corinthians 13:12—
"Greet one another with a holy kiss."**

©2001 Jonny Hawkins

Heckler: Christianity hasn't done much good. It's been in the world for two thousand years, and look at the mess we're in.

Preacher: Soap has been in the world longer than that, and look at the dirt on your face.

Christmas

Sign in big store: Five Santas, no waiting.

Jesus washed the disciples' feet.
Jesus cleanses us when we leave our souls
at the foot of the cross.

©2002 Jonny Hawkins

◉ ◉ ◉

You can tell you're growing old if you can remember
when you didn't start to shop for Christmas until
after Thanksgiving.

◉ ◉ ◉

Sign on church door: Please open before Christmas.

⊚ ⊚ ⊚

It is good to be children sometimes, and never better
    than at Christmas, when its mighty Founder was a
    child Himself.

—Charles Dickens

⊚ ⊚ ⊚

I passed one of those lots that sells Christmas trees.
    You know the kind. They're dedicated to the
    proposition that only God can make a tree and only
    man can make a buck!

⊚ ⊚ ⊚

There seems to be some question as to whether more
    gifts are exchanged on Christmas or the day
    after.

⊚ ⊚ ⊚

A little boy, excited about his part in the Christmas
    play, came home and said:

"I got a part in the Christmas play!"

"What part?" asked his mother.

"I'm one of the three wise guys!"

"I'm thinking of joining the
National Slingshot Association."

©2000 Jonny Hawkins

Church

Some go to church to take a walk;
Some go there to laugh and talk;
Some go there to meet a friend;
Some go there, their time to spend;
Some go there to meet a lover;
Some go there, a fault to cover;
Some go there for speculation;
Some go there for observation;
Some go there to doze and nod;
The wise go there to worship God.

◎ ◎ ◎

A church garden:

Three rows of squash

    1. Squash indifference.

    2. Squash criticism.

    3. Squash gossip.

Four rows of turnips

    1. Turn up for meetings.

    2. Turn up with a smile.

    3. Turn up with a visitor.

    4. Turn up with a Bible.

Five rows of lettuce

    1. Let us love one another.

    2. Let us welcome strangers.

    3. Let us be faithful to duty.

    4. Let us truly worship God.

    5. Let us give liberally.

◎ ◎ ◎

A church advertised for a new pastor by giving the character qualities they desired. Our new pastor must have:

- The strength of an eagle.
- The grace of a swan.
- The quiet beauty of a dove.

"Oh look...shepherd pie!"

©2001 Jonny Hawkins

- The keen eyesight of a hawk.
- The night hours of an owl.
- The friendliness of a sparrow.
- The industry of a woodpecker.
- The beauty of a gander.
- The attractiveness of a peacock.

After applying for the job, a certain minister walked out of the interview and wrote the following on the poster, "And when they get the bird they want—they want him to live on the food of a canary!"

Noah's Art

©2001 Jonny Hawkins

Church Attenders

A Dictionary of Church Attenders

Pillars: Worship regularly, giving time and money

Leaners: Use the church for funerals, baptisms, and weddings

Specials: Help and give occasionally for something that appeals to them

Annuals: Dress up for Easter and come for Christmas programs

Sponges: Take all blessing and benefits, even the sacraments, but never give out anything themselves

Scrappers: Take offense and criticize

Church Members

It seems that some church members have been starched and ironed, but too few have been washed.

First pastor: I hear you had a revival.

Second pastor: Yes, we did.

First pastor: How many additions did you have?

Second pastor: Oh, we didn't have any additions. But we had some blessed subtractions.

Church Signs

If Some People Lived Up to Their Ideals,
They Would Be Stooping

"I think so. I got a raspberry sliding into second base for the church softball team."

Everything You Always Wanted to Know
About Heaven and Hell
But Were Afraid to Ask

   ⑥ ⑥ ⑥

It Is More Blessed to Give Than to Receive
Besides—You Don't Have to Write Thank-You Notes

   ⑥ ⑥ ⑥

Try Our Sundays
They're Better than Baskin-Robbins

   ⑥ ⑥ ⑥

How Will You Spend Eternity?
Smoking or Non-smoking?

   ⑥ ⑥ ⑥

The Best Vitamin for a Christian Is B1

   ⑥ ⑥ ⑥

Under the Same Management for More than 2,000
 years

   ⑥ ⑥ ⑥

Soul Food Served Here

☺ ☺ ☺

Tithe if You Love Jesus!
Anyone Can Honk!

☺ ☺ ☺

Beat the Christmas Rush,
Come to Church this Sunday!

☺ ☺ ☺

Don't Give Up,
Moses Was Once a Basket Case

☺ ☺ ☺

Life Has Many Choices
Eternity Has Two
What's Yours?

☺ ☺ ☺

Worry Is Interest Paid on Trouble Before It Is Due

"You must be losin' it, Balaam.
Who ever heard of a talking donkey?"

©2000 Jonny Hawkins

ⓖ ⓖ ⓖ

Wal-Mart Isn't the Only Saving Place!

ⓖ ⓖ ⓖ

Preach the Gospel at All Times
Use Words If Necessary.

ⓖ ⓖ ⓖ

Prevent Truth Decay
Brush Up on Your Bible!

ⓖ ⓖ ⓖ

It's Hard to Stumble
When You're Down on Your Knees

ⓖ ⓖ ⓖ

What Part of 'THOU SHALT NOT'
Don't You Understand?

ⓖ ⓖ ⓖ

A Clear Conscience Makes a Soft Pillow

ⓖ ⓖ ⓖ

Can't Sleep? Try Counting Your Blessings

ⓖ ⓖ ⓖ

To Belittle Is to Be Little

⊚ ⊚ ⊚

God Answers Knee-Mail

⊚ ⊚ ⊚

Come In and Let Us Help Prepare You for Your Finals

⊚ ⊚ ⊚

What On Earth Are You Doing for Heaven's Sake?

⊚ ⊚ ⊚

Be Careful How You Live
You May Be the Only Bible
Some People Will Ever Read

⊚ ⊚ ⊚

Committees

To get something done, a committee should consist of three people, two of whom are absent.

⊚ ⊚ ⊚

Possible books read by Children of Israel

©2001 Jonny Hawkins

Committee is a noun of multitude signifying many but not signifying much.

A certain congregation was about to erect a new church edifice. The building committee, in consecutive meetings, passed the following resolutions:

1. We shall build a new church.

2. The new building is to be located on the site of the old one.

3. The material in the old building is to be used in the new one.

4. We shall continue to use the old building until the new one is completed.

Conclusion

A "second wind" is what some preachers get when they say, "And now in conclusion..."

Congregation

A minister looked out over his congregation and saw many people were not in attendance.

"Well, it looks like too many of our members are sack-religious this morning."

ⓖ ⓖ ⓖ

1st Pastor: Why did you resign from your church?

2nd Pastor: Because of illness and fatigue. The congregation was sick and tired of me.

Conscience

A guilty conscience is a hell on earth and points to one beyond.

ⓖ ⓖ ⓖ

**The Children of Israel's children
build a sandman in the wilderness**

All too often a clear conscience is merely the result of a bad memory.

Coughing

Preacher: A lot of people must be sick with colds. There was a lot of coughing during my sermon this morning.

Deacon: Those were time signals.

Count

Question: What happened when the man counting the people for King David went on vacation?

Answer: He took leave of his census.

"I'm confused. What do we call ourselves—the Children
of Israel, the Jews, the Canaanites, the Hebrews,
or the Moral Majority?!"

©2001 Jonny Hawkins

D
~ ~ ~

David

Question: What was the giveaway to David's
occupation when he was fleeing from King Saul?

Answer: The people knew he was a shepherd. David
was on the lam.

Dead Cat

A young mother was trying to comfort her daughter
after her pet kitten died. "Remember, dear,
Fluffy is up in heaven now with God."

"But Mommy," the girl sobbed. "What in the world
would God want with a dead cat?"

Denominations

Several churches in the South decided to hold union
services. The leader was a Baptist and proud of
his denomination.

"How many Baptists are here?" he asked on the first
night of the revival.

All except one little lady raised their hands.

"Lady, what are you?" asked the leader.

"I'm a Methodist," meekly replied the lady.

"Why are you a Methodist?" queried the leader.

"Well," replied the little old lady, "my grandparents were Methodists, my mother was a Methodist, and my late husband was a Methodist."

"Well," retorted the leader, "just supposing all your relatives had been morons, what would that have made you?"

"Oh, I see." The lady replied meekly, "A Baptist, I suppose."

ⓢ ⓢ ⓢ

A Methodist and a Baptist were arguing the virtues of their baptisms. The Methodist said, "All right, if I take a man and lead him in the water to his ankles, is he baptized?"

"No."

"Till just the top of his head is showing above the water—is he baptized?"

"No," said the Baptist. "His head must get wet."

"All right, then," asserted the Methodist. "That's where we baptize him."

ⓢ ⓢ ⓢ

How many Southern Baptists does it take to change a light bulb?

15,738,283. But they can't agree if it really needs to be changed.

**Blessed are the weeping willows,
for they shall be comforted.**

©2001 Jonny Hawkins

⊚ ⊚ ⊚

How many Campfire worship leaders does it take to change a light bulb?

One. But soon all can warm up to its glowing.

⊚ ⊚ ⊚

How many Mennonites does it take to change a light bulb?

Eventually about five, but they can get along fine without it.

⊚ ⊚ ⊚

How many televangelists does it take to change a light bulb?

Only one, but for the light to continue burning, you need to send in your check today.

⊚ ⊚ ⊚

How many Mormon missionaries does it take to change a light bulb?

Two. One to stand on the ladder while the other one rides his bike to the hardware store to get a bulb.

⊚ ⊚ ⊚

How many Episcopalians does it take to change a light bulb?

Three. One to do it, one to bless the element, and one to pour the sherry.

@ @ @

How many Nazarenes does it take to change a light bulb?

Eleven. One to change it and ten to organize the fellowship supper that follows.

@ @ @

How many Presbyterians does it take to change a light bulb?

They're not sure, but there are several committees studying the issue.

@ @ @

How many members of the Church of Christ does it take to change a light bulb?

Only one, but if anyone else tries to do it, the light won't come on.

@ @ @

©2001 Jonny Hawkins

How many Christian Scientists does it take to change a light bulb?

Three. One to talk to the light bulb and two to pray that the bulb will heal itself from within.

How many Methodists does it take to change a light bulb?

Only one, but first they want to make sure no one will be offended by the change.

⊚ ⊚ ⊚

How many Catholics does it take to change a light bulb?

Nine. One to change it and eight to sell raffle tickets for the old bulb.

⊚ ⊚ ⊚

How many Charismatics does it take to change a light bulb?

Three. One to do it, and two to bind the spirit of darkness.

⊚ ⊚ ⊚

How many Jehovah's Witnesses does it take to change a light bulb?

Two. One to change the light bulb and one to hand you some literature to read first before they change the bulb.

⊚ ⊚ ⊚

How many Amish does it take to change a light bulb?

What is a light bulb?

◎ ◎ ◎

In Texas, it got so hot that the Baptists were sprinkling, the Presbyterians were using a damp cloth, and the Episcopalians were giving rain checks.

Devil

A man was going to a Halloween party dressed in a costume of the devil. On his way it began to rain, so he darted into a church where a revival meeting happened to be in progress.

At the sight of his devil's costume, people began to scatter through the doors and windows.

One lady got her coat sleeve caught on the arm of one of the seats. As the man came closer, she pleaded: "Satan, I've been a member of this church for 20 years, but I've really been on your side all the time."

◎ ◎ ◎

While a revival was being conducted by a muscular preacher, he was disturbed by several young men that scoffed at everything they saw or heard.

He paused and asked them why they attended the meeting.

"We came to see miracles performed," impudently replied one of them.

Leaving the pulpit and walking quietly down the aisle, the minister seized one after the other by the collar and, as they disappeared out of the door, remarked:

"We don't perform miracles here, but we do cast out devils."

Divorce

America still has more marriages than divorces, proving that preachers can still outtalk lawyers.

Drinking

Drinker: What pastoral advice have you for drivers who drink?

Pastor: Jug not lest ye be jugged.

Dying

Old Pete was very close to dying but made a miraculous recovery. His pastor came to visit him in the hospital and the conversation went like this:

"Tell me, Pete, when you were so near death's door, did you feel afraid to meet your Maker?"

"No, Pastor," said Pete. "It was the other man I was afraid of!"

Last minute detail checks for the wise men

E
~~~

Elisha

Question: What special words did Elisha say to the man who lost his tool in the water?

Answer: Don't ax me!

Mark Twain was fond of telling the story of a small boy's account of Elisha and the prophet's less ingratiating mood.

"There was a prophet named Elisha. One day he was going up a mountainside. Some boys threw stones at him. He said, 'If you keep throwing stones at me, I'll set the bears on you and they'll eat you up.' And they did, and he did, and the bears did."

Epistles

Sunday school teacher: What are epistles?

Sunday school student: I guess they are the wives of the apostles.

"That's so far out of context, I could just vomit!...
and then return to it."

Evangelist

An evangelist was speaking in a meeting when a heckler shouted, "Listen to him...his father used to drive a wagon led by a donkey!"

"That's right," said the evangelist, "and today my father and the wagon are gone. But I see we still have the donkey with us."

Evil

To plan evil is as wrong as doing it.

—Proverbs 24:8

⑥ ⑥ ⑥

Supervising evil does not make it good.

Ezekiel

Question: When Ezekiel spoke to the people after lying on his side for a year and a half, why didn't the people listen to him?

Answer: They thought he was lying.

ENOCH WALKED WITH GOD.

ERNIE JUST SLEEPWALKED WITH HIS DOG.

F
~~~

Faith

If it weren't for faith, there would be no living in this world; we couldn't even eat hash with any safety.

—Josh Billings

⑤ ⑤ ⑤

An old European monastery is perched high on a 500-foot cliff. Visitors ride up in a big basket, pulled to the top with a ragged old rope.

Halfway up, a passenger nervously asked, "How often do you change the rope?"

The monk in charge replied, "Whenever the old one breaks."

Family

When the family returned from Sunday morning service father criticized the sermon, daughter thought the choir's singing was off-key, and mother found fault with the organist's playing. The subject had to be dropped when the small boy of the family said, "But it was a good show for a nickel, don't you think, Dad?"

"Paul, how did you get the scales
removed from your eyes?"

©2001 Jonny Hawkins

Fishing

Two men fishing on Sunday morning were feeling
   pretty guilty, especially since the fish didn't bite.
   One said to the other, "I guess I should have
   stayed home and gone to church."

To which the other angler replied lazily, "I couldn't
   have gone to church anyway—my wife's sick in
   bed."

Flavor

Question: From what Bible verse do we discover that
   God likes flavoring for food?

Answer: "To everything there is a season."

Forgiveness

Always forgive your enemies—nothing annoys them so
   much.

—Oscar Wilde

ⓖ ⓖ ⓖ

Forgiveness is the fragrance the violet sheds on the
   heel that has crushed it.

—Mark Twain

ⓖ ⓖ ⓖ

Forgiving the unrepentant is like drawing pictures on
   water.

ⓖ ⓖ ⓖ

"Oh...it's nice to see you're now putting on a happy face when you fast."

©2001 Jonny Hawkins

The weak can never forgive. Forgiveness is the attribute of the strong.

—Mahatma Gandhi

Freedom

Man is really free only in God, the source of his freedom.

—Sherwood Eddy

◎ ◎ ◎

To some people religious freedom means the choice of churches that they may stay away from.

Funeral

The preacher of a small church in a remote section of the country once preached a funeral service of one of the local mountaineers. He explained the deceased's position in the community in the following way:

"Now, he wasn't what you call a good man because he never gave his heart to the Lord, but he was what you'd call a respected sinner."

©2000 Jonny Hawkins

G
~~~

Giving

A miser is a rich pauper.

◎ ◎ ◎

Someone asked, "What is the most sensitive nerve in the human body?"

The preacher answered, "The one that leads to the pocketbook."

◎ ◎ ◎

In the ruins of an old church, excavators found a queerly shaped basket filled with buttons. It must have been a collection plate.

◎ ◎ ◎

When the usher came up the aisle with the basket at the offertory, a five-year-old boy in the front pew turned to his father and said loudly and excitedly, "Daddy, here comes the penny man!"

◎ ◎ ◎

"I lost the coat you gave me, so now
I'm going to sue the shirt off your back!"

©2001 Jonny Hawkins

Mother: Quick, Henry, call the doctor! Johnny just swallowed a coin!

Father: I think we ought to send for the minister. He can get money out of anybody.

⊚ ⊚ ⊚

Some people who give the Lord credit are reluctant to give Him cash.

—Jack Herbert

⊚ ⊚ ⊚

Minister before the morning offering: "The Lord owns the cattle on a thousand hills. He only needs cowboys to round them up. Will the ushers please come forward for the offering?"

⊚ ⊚ ⊚

Offering: A function in which many persons take only a passing interest.

God

He who leaves God out of his reckoning does not know how to count.

⊚ ⊚ ⊚

"False prophets come in sheep's clothing?
I didn't even know sheep <u>wore</u> clothes!"

©2001 Jonny Hawkins

He who does not believe that God is above all is either a fool or has no experience of life.

—Caecilius Statius

Goliath

Question: What song did David sing when he went out to fight the giant Goliath?

Answer: "Of Thee I Sling."

Golden Rule

"Always remember we are here to help others," said a mother as she explained the Golden Rule.

Her little one thought for a moment and inquired, "Well, what are the others here for?"

Golf

Friend: Pastor, how do you let off steam when you miss a shot and your ball goes into a sand trap?

Pastor: I just repeat the names of some of the members of my congregation...with great feeling!

The last time I sang in church the pastor told me it would be okay for me to play golf on Sundays.

Goodness

Sin writes histories, goodness is silent.

—Goethe

Gossip

Did you hear about the pastor who spoke on gossip and then for his closing song chose, "I Love to Tell the Story"?

H

Halo

A halo has to fall only 11 inches to become a noose.

Health Care

Here is a sample of what might happen if the liberal Health Care Plan especially designed for church pastors would pass Congress:

An average middle-class pastor who was feeling the need of medical care went to the approved medical building. He entered and took an elevator to the ninth floor. Upon leaving the elevator, he found himself faced with a battery of doors, each marked with the names of ailments such as appendicitis, heart, cancer, etc.

He felt sure his trouble could be diagnosed as appendicitis, so he entered the door so marked. Upon entering, he found himself faced with two more doors, one marked "male" and the other "female." He entered the door marked "male" and found himself in another corridor. Here he found two doors, one marked "Protestant" and the other "Catholic."

Since he was a Protestant, he entered the proper door and found himself facing two more doors. The first door was marked "taxpayer" and the

other "non-taxpayer." He still owned equity in his home, so he went through the door marked "taxpayer" and found himself confronted with two more doors marked "single" and "married."

He had a wife at home, so he entered the proper door and once more there were two more doors. One marked "Republican" and the other "Democrat."

BECAUSE HE WAS A REPUBLICAN, HE ENTERED THAT DOOR AND FELL NINE FLOORS TO THE ALLEY.

Hearing

The world is dying for want—not of good preaching, but of good hearing.

—George Dana Boardman

Heart

When God measures a man, He puts the tape around the heart instead of the head.

Heaven

A new group of male applicants had just arrived in heaven.

Peter looked them over and ordered, "All men who were henpecked on earth, please step to the left. All those who were bosses in their own home, step to the right."

"I didn't appreciate your subtle reference to me in your sermon on being unequally yoked.

©2000 Jonny Hawkins

The line quickly formed to the left. Only one man stepped to the right.

Peter looked at the frail little man standing by himself and inquired, "What makes you think you belong on that side?"

Without hesitation, the meek little man explained, "This is where my wife told me to stand."

⑥ ⑥ ⑥

**"I'd like an order of surf and turf...
and supersize it!"**

©2001 Jonny Hawkins

"It's tough living out the fruit of the Spirit when my flesh just wants to be a couch potato."

©2001 Jonny Hawkins

If I ever reach heaven, I expect to find three wonders there: First, to meet some I had not thought to see there; second, to miss some I had expected to see there; and third, the greatest wonder of all, to find myself there.

—John Newton

A woman arrived at the gates of heaven. While she was waiting for Saint Peter to greet her, she peeked through the gates and saw a beautiful banquet table. Sitting all around were her parents and all the other people she had loved and who had died before her. They saw her and began calling greetings to her:

"Hello—How are you?"

"We've been waiting for you!"

"Good to see you!"

When Saint Peter came by, the woman said to him, "This is such a wonderful place! How do I get in?"

"You have to spell a word," Saint Peter told her.

"Which word?" the woman asked.

"Love."

The woman correctly spelled "love" and Saint Peter welcomed her into heaven. About a year later, Saint Peter came to the woman and asked her to watch the gates of heaven for him that day. While the woman was guarding the gates of heaven, her husband arrived.

"I'm surprised to see you," the woman said. "How have you been?"

"Oh, I've been doing really well since you died," her husband told her.

"Do you remember that beautiful young nurse who was taking care of you in the hospital? Well, I married her and she was very special. Then we won the multi-state lottery. I sold the little house we used to live in, and bought a huge mansion. In fact, several homes. My new wife and I began to travel the world having a wonderful time together. While on vacation in Cancun, I went waterskiing. In fact, it was today. I fell and hit my head, and here I am. What a bummer! How do I get in?"

"All you have to do is spell one word!" the woman told him.

"What's the word?" her husband asked.

"Czechoslovakia."

Hell

While training young ministers to preach, Charles Spurgeon gave them this advice:

"When you speak of heaven," he said, "let your face light up with a heavenly gleam. Let your eyes shine with reflected glory. And when you speak of hell...well, then your everyday face will do."

⊚   ⊚   ⊚

An automobile accident had rendered one motorist unconscious. As he was being carried away, he opened his eyes and began to struggle desperately to get away. Afterward, he explained that the first thing he saw was a "Shell" sign, and somebody was standing in front of the "S."

⊚   ⊚   ⊚

Adam's new garment made from fruit of the doom.

©2001 Jonny Hawkins

If there is no hell, a good many preachers are
   obtaining money under false pretenses.

—William A. Sunday

ⓖ ⓖ ⓖ

Hell is truth seen too late, duty neglected in its
   season.

—Tryon Edwards

ⓖ ⓖ ⓖ

"**What does it say about the Great <u>German</u> Shepherd laying down his life for his sheep?**"

God continues to think outside the box (we try to put Him in).

Moses and the water hazard

©2000 Jonny Hawkins

A woman dreamed that she was talking with her late
 husband, "Are you happy now?" she asked him.

"Very."

"Happier than you were on earth with me? Tell me,
 darling, what's it like in heaven?"

"Who said I was in heaven?"

"If you don't get a percentage on each conversion, then what is all this I hear about the great commission?"

©2002 Jonny Hawkins

Humility

Nothing sets a person so much out of the devil's reach as humility.

—Jonathan Edwards

Hymn

Instead of singing the Doxology phrase, "Praise Him, all creatures here below," a little girl sang, "Praise Him, all preachers, here we go." It made sense to her because everybody sang it at the end of the service, just as they were leaving.

⑥　⑥　⑥

A song leader who had not carefully considered the words of the song he was leading said, "I want the women to sing the verse, 'I will go home today,' and the men to come in on the chorus with 'Glad day, Glad day.'" The people were laughing too much to sing the song.

⑥　⑥　⑥

Question: What is the most appropriate of all songs for the choir to sing just after the morning sermon?
Answer: "Awake, Ye Sinners."

Otherwise known as "Hem and Haw"

©2001 Jonny Hawkins

I

Immerse

Conversion by Baptist standards requires that you go from bad to immerse.

Interrupt

Member to pastor at the end of the morning service: "Pastor, you were really good this morning! You interrupted my thoughts at least half a dozen times!"

The grass is always greener
when you're sittin' on the fence.

©2000 Jonny Hawkins.

J
~~~

Jericho

Question: What special food was first created in Jericho?

Answer: Wall fall.

Jesus

Question: What caused Jesus to perform a miracle at the wedding in Cana?

Answer: His mother was wine-ing.

Job

Question: Why was Job always cold in bed?

Answer: Because he had such miserable comforters.

⊚ ⊚ ⊚

Question: Who was the most successful physician in the Bible?

Answer: Job. He had the most patience.

Upon leaving an inhospitable city, one of the disciples shakes Dusty off his heels.

©2001 Jonny Hawkins

John the Baptist

Question: How did John the Baptist act when he was about to be killed?

Answer: He lost his head.

Jonah

Question: How did Jonah feel when the great fish swallowed him?

Answer: Down in the mouth.

ⓖ ⓖ ⓖ

A lady turned to her young son and said, "Did you enjoy Pastor Phillips' sermon about Jonah and the whale?"

"I guess so," the boy said. "But I feel just like that whale. All that preaching's given me a bellyache."

ⓖ ⓖ ⓖ

Pastor: Just think of it, Jonah spent three days in the belly of a large fish.

Member: That's nothing, my husband spent longer than that in the belly of an alligator.

Pastor: Well, I declare...just how long was he in there?

Member: It's almost four years, now.

Joseph

Question: How did Joseph feel when his brothers threw him in a well?

Answer: It was the pits.

@ @ @

Question: What were Joseph's thoughts about the cupbearer who forgot about him while he was in prison?

Answer: "E-gypt me!"

Judge

A lady was showing a church friend her neighbor's wash through her back window.

"Our neighbor isn't very clean. Look at those streaks on the wash!"

Her friend replied, "Those streaks aren't on your neighbor's wash. They're on your window."

Judgment Day

"There will be thunder, lightning, flood, fires, and earthquakes!" roared the preacher, describing Judgment Day.

Wide-eyed, a little boy in the congregation tugged at his mother's sleeve: "Will I get out of school?"

K

Knock Knock

Knock, knock.
Who's there?
Ach.
Ach who?
God bless you.

Knock, knock.
Who's there?
Owl.
Owl who?
Owl be seeing you.

Knock, knock.
Who's there?
Noah.
Noah who?
Noah a good place to eat around here?

©2001 Jonny Hawkins

Laughter

Of all the things God created, I am often most
grateful He created laughter.

—Charles Swindoll

⑥ ⑥ ⑥

Laughter is the closest thing to the grace of God.

—Karl Barth

⑥ ⑥ ⑥

If you're not allowed to laugh in heaven, I don't want
to go there.

—Martin Luther

⑥ ⑥ ⑥

Laughter is the shortest distance between two people.

—Victor Borge

"Job, I'm prescribing sterilized shards of pottery to scrape these boils."

©2001 Jonny Hawkins

Lionize

Lionize: What the Romans did to the early Christians.

Lord's Prayer

Children's versions of the Lord's Prayer:

—Our Father, who are in heaven, hello! What be Thy name?

—Give us this day our daily breath.

—Our Father, who are in heaven, Hollywood be Thy name.

—Give us this day our jelly bread.

—Lead us not into creation.

—Deliver us from weevils.

—Deliver us from eagles.

Two lawyers were bosom buddies. Much to the amazement of one, the other became a Sunday school teacher. "I bet you don't even know the Lord's Prayer," the first one fumed.

"Everybody knows that," the other replied. "It's 'Now I lay me down to sleep.'"

"You win," said the first one admiringly. "I didn't know you knew so much about the Bible."

"Jonah, I didn't realize you had a green thumb...
and arm...and face..."

Lot

Question: What caused Lot's wife to be so well known?

Answer: She became a pillar of the community.

ⓢ   ⓢ   ⓢ

The Sunday school teacher was describing how Lot's wife looked back and suddenly turned into a pillar of salt.

"My mother looked back once while she was driving," contributed little Willie. "She turned into a telephone pole."

"One request, Lord. Any chance
you could make this a laser pointer?"

M

Marriage

Man: Pastor, do you think it is right for one man to profit from another man's mistake?

Pastor: Why, most certainly not!

Man: Then would you mind returning the $50 I gave you last year for performing my wedding?

◎　◎　◎

A man went to see his minister about some marital problems.

Minister: Just what is the problem?

Member: I think my wife is trying to poison me!

Minister: I don't think that is possible.

Member: I'm telling you. I'm certain she's trying to poison me. What should I do?

Minister: Tell you what. Let me talk to her, I'll see what I can find out and I'll let you know.

A week passes and the pastor contacts the member.

Minister: Well, I spoke to your wife. I was on the phone for three hours. You want my advice?

Member: Yes, of course!

Minister: Take the poison!

"It's manna. It's rich in protein
and high in moral fiber."

©2000 Jonny Hawkins

The new loudspeaker system recently installed in the
church has been given by Mr. MacArthur in
memory of his wife.

Martha

Question: What was Martha's attitude about doing all
the work in the kitchen?

Answer: She wasn't merry about it.

Matthew

Question: What did Matthew use on his bulletin board?

Answer: Tax.

Methuselah

Methuselah ate what he found on his plate,
　　And never, as people do now,
Did he note the amount of the calorie count;
　　He ate it because it was chow.
He wasn't disturbed as at dinner he sat,
　　Devouring a roast or a pie,
To think it was lacking in granular fat
　　Or a couple of vitamins shy.
He cheerfully chewed each species of food,
　　Unmindful of troubles or fears
Lest his health might be hurt
　　By some fancy dessert;
And he lived over nine hundred years.

Milk and Honey

Sunday school teacher: What do you think the land "flowing with milk and honey" was like?

Sunday school student: Sticky!

Mary and Joseph travel to Bethlehem.

©2001 Jonny Hawkins

Minister

"How do you like the new minister?" a customer asked one of the merchants in town.

"I haven't heard him preach, but I like him fine," said the merchant.

"How can that be if you don't know him?"

"Oh, I can tell how good he is—the people are beginning to pay up their bills," said the merchant.

ⓖ ⓖ ⓖ

JOSHUA AND HIS TRUMPETERS

©2001 Jonny Hawkins

Delivering a speech at a banquet on the night of his arrival in a large city, a visiting minister told several anecdotes he expected to repeat at meetings the next day.

Because he wanted to use the jokes again, he requested the reporters to omit them from any accounts they might turn in to their newspapers.

A cub reporter, in commenting on the speech, ended his piece with the following: "The minister told a number of stories that cannot be published."

Ministers fall into four categories:

1. Those who do not have any notes, and the people have no idea how long they will speak.
2. Those who set each page of their sermon on the podium as they read it. These honest ones enable the congregation to keep track of how much more is to come.
3. Those who cheat by putting each sheet of notes under the others in their hand.
4. And, worst of all, those who put down each sheet of notes as they read them and then horrify the audience by picking up the whole batch and reading the other side.

While the minister was speaking, a man fell asleep. The minister raised his voice and pounded the pulpit, but the man would not wake up. Finally, the minister called to a deacon, "Go wake that man up."

The deacon replied, "Wake him up yourself. You put him to sleep."

Prime minister: A preacher at his best.

Jesus turns water into wine.
Man turns the outpouring into whine.

Misbehave

After a spanking for being naughty, five-year-old
Mark was advised to tell God that he was sorry. At
bedtime, he folded his hands and explained to God
that Satan had tempted him to misbehave. Then
he turned to his mother and said, "God just told
me he's going to spank Satan in the morning."

And thus the mountain was so aptly named.

©2001 Jonny Hawkins

Moral Courage

A minister was speaking to a class of boys on the merits of moral courage. "Ten boys were sleeping in a dormitory," he said by way of illustration, "and only one knelt down to say his prayers. That is moral courage."

When he had finished his talk, he asked one boy to give him another example of moral courage.

One boy said, "Ten ministers were sleeping in a dormitory, and only one jumped into bed without saying his prayers."

James and John, "Sons of Thunder," give new meaning to the term "baby boomers."

Mordecai

Question: Why wasn't Mordecai hung on the gallows that Haman had made for him?

Answer: He just couldn't get the hang of it.

Moses

Question: Where is medicine first mentioned in the Bible?

Answer: When the Lord gives Moses two tablets.

◎ ◎ ◎

Question: Why did Moses cross the Red Sea?

Answer: To avoid Egyptian traffic.

◎ ◎ ◎

Teacher: Today our Bible story is about Moses and the plagues sent on the people of Egypt. Does anyone know what a plague is?

Student: Yes, my brother is one.

◎ ◎ ◎

1st Woman: Why do you think Moses wandered for forty years in the wilderness?

2nd Woman: He was like all men. He wouldn't stop and ask for directions.

©2001 Jonny Hawkins

N
~~~

New Age

Did you hear about the New Age church in California? It has three commandments and seven suggestions.

New Birth

One excuse often used for not becoming a Christian is, "I don't understand the new birth." Of course, not many people understand love, but they get married anyway.

Noah

Ned: What instructions did Noah give his sons about fishing off the ark?

Ted: I don't know.

Ned: Go easy on the bait, boys. I have only two worms.

ⓖ ⓖ ⓖ

Question: Who was the best financier in the Bible?

Answer: Noah—he floated his stock while the whole world was in liquidation.

Nehemiah in the dating years

©2001 Jonny Hawkins

◎ ◎ ◎

Question: Why didn't they play cards on Noah's ark?
Answer: Because Noah sat on the deck.

◎ ◎ ◎

Joe: Was there any money on Noah's ark?
Moe: Yes. The duck took a bill, the frog took a green-
back, and the skunk took a scent.

◎ ◎ ◎

One thing about Noah—he didn't miss the boat.

◎ ◎ ◎

Teacher: Do you know who built the ark?
Student: No!
Teacher: Correct.

◎ ◎ ◎

Noah was standing at the gangplank checking off the
pairs of animals, when he saw three camels trying
to get on board.

"Wait a minute!" said Noah, "Two each is the limit. One of you will have to stay behind."

"It won't be me," said the first camel. "I'm the camel whose back is broken by the last straw."

"I'm the one people swallow while straining out a gnat," said the second.

"I," said the third, "am the one that shall pass through the eye of a needle sooner than a rich man shall enter heaven."

"Come on in," said Noah, "the world is going to need all of you."

Nodding

"Did they like my sermon?" the anxious young minister asked his wife on their way home.

"I think so, dear," she replied tactfully. "At least they were all nodding."

Nursery

Sign above the door of the church nursery: *They shall not all sleep, but they shall all be changed.*

O
~~~

Offering

Mother: Now remember to put some of your allowance in the offering at church.

Son: Why not buy an ice cream cone with it and let the cashier put it in the offering?

ⓖ ⓖ ⓖ

The best test of your faith is when the collection plate comes around and the smallest you have is a twenty.

Organist

Generations ago, an organist wanted to impress a visiting clergyman with her musical accomplishment. She wrote a note to the old sexton who had been a little slack in his work of pumping enough air for the organ, and she handed it to him just before the service started.

Unfortunately, the sexton made a mistake. He passed the note on to the visiting clergyman, who opened it and read: Keep blowing away until I give the signal to stop.

"No, no, no...for the last time,
we're not interested in aluminum siding!"

©2001 Jonny Hawkins

P
~~~

Pastor

Clara: My pastor is so good he can talk on any subject for an hour.

Sarah: That's nothing! My pastor can talk for an hour about nothing.

ⓖ ⓖ ⓖ

Did you hear about the young pastor who fouled up the established routine? He didn't stand at the door and shake hands with the worshippers after the service. He went out to the curb and shook hands with the red-faced parents waiting for their children to come out of Sunday school.

ⓖ ⓖ ⓖ

One older pastor was talking to another elderly pastor. He was sharing that he had a difficult time in preparing sermons anymore. He said that he was having a hard time with today's language.

- Hardware used to refer to a store not computer equipment.

©2000 Jonny Hawkins

- Enter was a sign on a door, not a button on a computer keyboard, and chip was a piece of wood.
- Fast food was what you ate during Lent.
- Rock music, at one time, took place when grandma sang a lullaby in a rocking chair.

Paul

Question: Who carried the coffin when Paul died?

Answer: Paul bearers.

"I was made for the occasion...
I'm a thunder and lightning bug."

©2002 Jonny Hawkins

Pest

Wife: Who was that at the door, dear?

Husband: It was that new minister. He has been by four times this week.

Wife: What is his name?

Husband: I think it's Pester Smith.

Pharaoh

Question: How do we know that Pharaoh was in financial trouble?

Answer: He was in the Red, see.

Pious

A profoundly pious look will not cover a poorly prepared message.

Plans

If God is your partner, you had better make large plans.

Pledges

The deacon ran into the pastor's office and exclaimed excitedly, "Pastor, I have terrible news to report! Burglars must've broken in last night...they stole $90,000 worth of pledges!"

Practice

You know what's wrong with religion today? There are too many people practicing it—and not enough people good at it!

Prayer

Billy: What are prayers, anyway?

Mother: They are messages sent to heaven.

Billy: Well, do I pray at night because the rates are cheaper?

ⓖ ⓖ ⓖ

After attending a prayer meeting where everyone
   prayed very loud, a little boy remarked, "If they
   lived nearer to God, they wouldn't have to shout."

ⓖ ⓖ ⓖ

Little Jane, whose grandmother was visiting her
   family, was going to bed when her mother called:

"Don't forget to include Grandma in your prayers
   tonight. Ask God to bless her and let her live to be
   very, very old."

"She's old enough," replied Jane. "I'd rather pray that
   God would make her young."

ⓖ ⓖ ⓖ

Little Dennis began falling out of a tree and cried,
   "Lord, save me, save me!" There was a pause, and
   then he said, "Never mind, Lord. My pants just
   caught on a branch."

ⓖ ⓖ ⓖ

The pastor was invited to dinner and asked to lead in
   prayer for the meal. After a brief prayer, Junior
   said approvingly, "You don't pray so long when
   you're hungry, do you?"

"I don't know, Peter, I've never seen one like this before."

©2001 Jonny Hawkins

🌀 🌀 🌀

Mother: That's no way to say your prayers.

Daughter: But Mom, I thought that God was tired of hearing the same old stuff every night, so I told Him the story of the Three Bears instead.

🌀 🌀 🌀

The fewer the words, the better the prayer.

—Martin Luther

Non-fruits of the Spirit

©2001 Jonny Hawkins

ᛮ ᛮ ᛮ

Passenger: You drive the car and I'll pray.

Driver: What's the matter, don't you trust my driving?

Passenger: Of course I do! Don't you trust my praying?

ᛮ ᛮ ᛮ

The Christian on his knees sees more than the philosopher on his tiptoes.

Preach

The parson of a tiny congregation in Arkansas disappeared one night with the entire church treasury. Within a week, the local sheriff had captured him and brought him back to face his parishioners.

"Here's the varmint, folks," announced the sheriff grimly. "I'm sorry to say that he has squandered our money. I drug him back so we can make him preach it out."

Preacher

Preacher: Please take it easy on the bill for repairing my car. Remember, I am a poor preacher.

Mechanic: I know, I heard you on Sunday.

ᛮ ᛮ ᛮ

Non-fruits of the Spirit

After returning from church one Sunday a small boy said, "You know what, Mommy? I'm going to be a minister when I grow up."

"That's fine," said his mother. "But what made you decide you want to be a preacher?"

"Well," said the boy pensively, "I'll have to go to church on Sunday anyway, and I think it would be more fun to stand up and yell than to sit still and listen."

⑤　⑤　⑤

The ideal preacher...

- He preaches exactly 20 minutes and then sits down.
- He condemns sin but never hurts anyone's feelings.
- He works from 8:00 A.M. to 10:00 P.M. in every type of work from preaching to taxi service.
- He makes $60 a week, wears good clothes, buys good books regularly, has a nice family, drives a good car, and gives $30 a week to missions.
- He contributes to every good work that comes along.
- He is 26 years old and has been preaching for 30 years.
- He is tall and short, thin and heavyset, plain looking but handsome.

- He has one brown eye and one blue, hair parted in the middle, left side straight and dark, the other side wavy and blonde.
- He has a burning desire to work with teenagers and spends all his time with the older folks.
- He smiles all the time with a straight face because he has a sense of humor that keeps him seriously dedicated to his work.
- He makes 15 calls a day on church members, spends all his time evangelizing the unchurched, and is never out of his office.
- He is truly a remarkable person—and he does not exist.

◎ ◎ ◎

Boy: Awaking in church: "Daddy, has the preacher finished yet?"

Father: "Yep! He's finished, but he hasn't stopped talking."

◎ ◎ ◎

A nervous young preacher stood before the congregation to preach his first sermon. He was just out of seminary.

"F-f-f-friends, when I came here this morning only the Lord and myself knew what I was going to preach. And now only the Lord knows."

◎ ◎ ◎

What a preacher! His sermons were like water to a drowning man.

◎ ◎ ◎

He charged nothing for his preaching, and it was worth it.

—Mark Twain

Preaching

First preacher: I think a pastor needs to study diligently for his Sunday morning message.

Second preacher: I disagree. Many times I have no idea what I am going to preach about, but I go into the pulpit and preach and think nothing of it.

First preacher: You think nothing of it—and your deacons have told me they share your opinion.

Prodigal Son

Teacher: Who was sorry when the Prodigal Son returned home?

Student: The fatted calf.

◎ ◎ ◎

Non-fruits of the Spirit

"Melody in F" (The Prodigal Son)

Feeling footloose and frisky, a feather-brained fellow
Forced his fond father to fork over the farthings,
Flew far to foreign fields,
And frittered his fortune feasting fabulously with
    faithless friends.
Fleeced by his fellows in folly and facing famine,
He found himself a feed flinger in a filthy farm yard.
Fairly famishing, he fain would have filled his frame
With foraged food from fodder fragments.
"Phooey, my father's flunkies fare far finer,"
The frazzled fugitive fumbled, frankly facing fact.
Frustrated by failure and filled with foreboding,
He fled forthwith to his family.
Falling at his father's feet, he forlornly fumbled,
"Father, I've flunked
And fruitlessly forfeited family fellowship favor."
The farsighted father, forestalling further flinching,
Frantically flagged the flunkies to
Fetch a fatling from the flock and fix a feast.
The fugitive's faultfinding brother frowned
On fickle forgiveness of former folderol.
But the faithful father figured,
"Filial fidelity is fine, but the fugitive is found!
What forbids fervent festivity?
Let the flags be unfurled! Let fanfares flare!"

Father's forgiveness formed the foundation
For the former fugitive's future fortitude!

Prophets

Question: What is the favorite song for the Old Testament prophets?

Answer: "Hosea, can you see..."

Proverb

Proverb: A short sentence based on long experience.

Polygamy

What is the extreme punishment for having more than one wife? Having more than one mother-in-law.

Q
~~~

Quaker

A Quaker became exasperated with his cow for kicking over a pail of milk.

He warned, "You know, because of my religion, I can't punish you. But if you do that again, I'll sell you to a Baptist preacher, and he'll kick you so hard you'll never be able to kick that pail over again!"

Queen

Question: When is a queen like a mirror?

Answer: When she is a good-looking lass.

The Parable of the Sewer

©2002 Jonny Hawkins

R

Religion

It is the test of a good religion whether you can joke about it.

—G.K. Chesterton

Religion is the best armor in the world, but the worst cloak.

—John Bunyan

Revival

During a revival one of the town's worst sinners came forward to be baptized.

Sinner: I understand that I should be dipped.

Minister: I think we'll have to anchor you out here overnight.

Rich

It's hard for a rich man to enter the kingdom of heaven, but it's easy for him to get on the church board of trustees.

How Joseph really got his coat of many colors

©2001 Jonny Hawkins

"I like your beatitude!"

©2000 Jonny Hawkins

Riddle

Question: When was money first mentioned in the Bible?

Answer: When the dove brought the green back to the ark.

Question: Why are there so few men with whiskers in heaven?

Answer: Because most men get in by a close shave.

ⓢ ⓢ ⓢ

Question: How were the Egyptians paid for goods taken by the Israelites when they fled from Egypt?

Answer: The Egyptians got a check on the bank of the Red Sea.

ⓢ ⓢ ⓢ

Question: How do we know they used arithmetic in early Bible times?

Answer: Because the Lord said to multiply on the face of the earth.

ⓢ ⓢ ⓢ

Question: Why didn't the last dove return to the ark?

Answer: Because she had sufficient grounds to stay away.

ⓢ ⓢ ⓢ

Question: Who sounded the first bell in the Bible?

Answer: Cain, when he hit Abel.

"Your parable of the talents inspired me, Pastor.
I'm developing my gift of impersonations."

Romans

Question: Why did the Romans think Paul was an alcoholic?

Answer: He spent so much of his time behind bars.

ⓖ ⓖ ⓖ

First archaeologist: I still don't understand how the ancient Romans managed to build Rome so quickly.

Second archaeologist: They didn't take coffee breaks.

Salary

Friend: Say, Pastor, how is it that you're so thin and gaunt, but your horse is so fat and sleek?

Pastor: I feed the horse and the congregation feeds me.

Samson

Question: What did Samson think about his date with Delilah?

Answer: It was hair-raising.

ⓖ ⓖ ⓖ

A Sunday school teacher asked her class to write about the story of Samson. One teenage girl wrote, "Samson wasn't so unusual. The boys I know brag about their strength and wear their hair long, too."

Satan

Satan as a master is bad, his work is worse, and his wages are worst of all.

Sermon

The average man's idea of a good sermon is that it
   goes over his head—and hits one of his neighbors.

◎ ◎ ◎

One beautiful Sunday morning, a minister announced to
   his congregation: "I have here in my hands three
   sermons—a $100 sermon that lasts five minutes, a
   $50 sermon that lasts 15 minutes—and a $10
   sermon that lasts a full hour. Let's receive this
   morning's offering and see which one I'll deliver."

◎ ◎ ◎

A young preacher who lost his Sunday morning sermon
   notes told the congregation he would have to
   depend on the Lord for the message. He went on
   to inform the people that if they would come back
   in the evening, he would be better prepared.

◎ ◎ ◎

A sermon's length is not its strength.

◎ ◎ ◎

The tempting of Bill Gates

©2001 Jonny Hawkins

Member: Pastor, how did you get that cut on your face?

Pastor: I was thinking about my sermon this morning and cut myself shaving.

Member: That's too bad! Next time you had better concentrate on your shaving and cut your sermon.

☺ ☺ ☺

Billy Gilder sheepishly shares his faith.

©2001 Jonny Hawkins

One Sunday, a pastor noticed a member arrive very late during the 9:30 service. To his surprise, the member was in his seat when the 11:00 service began. But when the congregation rose to sing the hymn before the sermon, he left, explaining to the usher, "This is where I came in."

ⓢ ⓢ ⓢ

Rocking Horse sermon: Back and forth, back and forth, but going nowhere

Mockingbird sermon: Repetition, nothing new

Smorgasbord sermon: A little bit of everything, but nothing solid

Jericho sermon: March around the subject seven times

Christmas Tree sermon: Something offered for nothing

ⓢ ⓢ ⓢ

Member: How did you like the minister's sermon?

Friend: Well, frankly, I like our own minister better.

Member: Why is that?

Friend: It's the words they use. Our minister says, "In conclusion," and then he concludes. Your minister says, "Lastly," and he lasts.

ⓢ ⓢ ⓢ

Good evening, ladies and gentlemen. You'll be glad to know that when I asked my secretary to type this sermon out for me...I asked her to eliminate anything that was dull or confusing. So in conclusion...

Sin

A minister told his congregation that there were 739 different sins. He immediately received 80 requests for the list.

ⓖ ⓖ ⓖ

A nice, but blundering, old lady liked the new pastor and wanted to compliment him as she was leaving church after service. She told him, "I must say, we folks didn't know what sin was until you took charge of our parish."

ⓖ ⓖ ⓖ

Sunday school teacher: What must we do before we can receive the forgiveness of sins?

Student: We must sin.

ⓖ ⓖ ⓖ

Many people develop a split personality because they try to be a sinner and a saint at the same time.

—Herbert A. Streeter

ⓖ ⓖ ⓖ

"So, I'm adored by the Father, the Son, <u>and</u> the Holy Spirit? It sounds like an unconditional love triangle."

©2002 Jonny Hawkins

There is no more "original sin." No matter how unusual it is, it has been thought of before by thousands.

ⓢ ⓢ ⓢ

Few sinners are saved after the first twenty minutes of a sermon.

—Mark Twain

Sleep

As they were leaving church one Sunday, a man confided to his friend he was suffering from insomnia. The friend asserted he had no trouble getting to sleep.

"Really?" he inquired. "Do you count sheep?"

"No," was the retort, "I talk to the Shepherd."

ⓢ ⓢ ⓢ

A parishioner had dozed off to sleep during the morning service.

"Will all who want to go to heaven stand?" the preacher asked.

All stood except the sleeping parishioner.

After they sat down, the pastor continued: "Well, will all who want to go to the other place stand?"

Someone suddenly dropped a songbook, and the sleeping man jumped to his feet and stood sheepishly facing the preacher. "I don't know what we're voting for, but it looks like you and I are the only ones for it."

⊚ ⊚ ⊚

If all the people who sleep in church were laid end-to-end, they'd be a lot more comfortable.

Snoring

"Did you hear Robinson snoring in church this morning? It was simply awful."

"Yes, I did—he woke me up."

Solomon

Question: Why did King Solomon decide to build the Temple?

Answer: He had an edifice complex.

⊚ ⊚ ⊚

Question: Where was Solomon's temple located?

Answer: On the side of his head.

⊚ ⊚ ⊚

Question: What was King Solomon's answer to the two women when each claimed that the same baby belonged to her?

Answer: It was a split decision.

Songs

Favorite Songs of Bible Characters

NOAH: Raindrops Keep Falling on My Head

ADAM: Strangers in Paradise

LAZARUS: The Second Time Around

JOB: I've Got a Right to Sing the Blues

MOSES: The Wanderer

SAMSON: Hair

DANIEL: The Lion Sleeps Tonight

JOSHUA: Good Vibrations

ELIJAH: Up, Up, and Away

METHUSELAH: Stayin' Alive

Spank

After administering a spanking, a father returned to his son's room to talk with him. "I really didn't want to spank you, but the Bible says that children should obey their parents."

"I know," was the tearful reply, "but the Bible says, 'Be ye kind one to another,' too."

"Maybe Paul had a thorn in the flesh
because he kicked the prickles."

©2001 Jonny Hawkins

Sunday

Question: What is the strongest day in the week?

Answer: Sunday. The rest are weak days.

Sunday School

Sunday school teacher: Where can you find the Beatitudes?

Sunday school student: Have you tried the Yellow Pages?

◎ ◎ ◎

Son: Dad, did you go to Sunday school when you were young?

Dad: Never missed a Sunday.

Son: Bet it won't do me any good either.

◎ ◎ ◎

Sunday school teacher: Why do you believe in God?

Small student: I guess it just runs in our family.

◎ ◎ ◎

A Sunday school teacher asked her students to draw a picture of the holy family. After the pictures were brought to her, she saw that some of the youngsters had drawn the conventional pictures—the holy family and the manger, the holy family riding on the mule, etc.

But she called up one little boy to ask him to explain his drawing, which showed an airplane with four heads sticking out of the plane windows.

She said, "I can understand you drew three of the heads to show Joseph, Mary, and Jesus. But who's the fourth head?"

"Oh," answered the boy, "that's Pontius, the pilot!"

ⓢ ⓢ ⓢ

Teacher: Johnny, you shouldn't talk so loudly in Sunday school.

Johnny: Billy Graham does!

ⓢ ⓢ ⓢ

Teacher: Why would it be wrong to cut off a cat's tail?

Student: The Bible says, "What God has joined together, let no man put asunder."

ⓢ ⓢ ⓢ

"But I'm already the caterpillar of the community."

©2002 Jonny Hawkins

"I cried at Sunday school," the boy reported to his mother after surviving his first session.

"Why did you cry?"

"I looked around the room, and I was the only guy there I knew!"

⊚ ⊚ ⊚

One six-year-old boy wrote, "My favorite Bible story is the one where the plowshares are turned into Fords."

⊚ ⊚ ⊚

Question: What does the story of Jonah and the great fish teach us?

Answer: You can't keep a good man down.

⊚ ⊚ ⊚

Question: Which came first, the chicken or the egg?

Answer: The chicken, of course. God couldn't lay an egg.

T
~~~

Temptation

The road to success is dotted with many tempting
parking places.

☺ ☺ ☺

When you flee temptation, be sure you don't leave a
forwarding address.

Ten Commandments

As Moses said to the multitude when he showed them
the Ten Commandments, "You might say they're
nonnegotiable demands."

☺ ☺ ☺

When a Sunday school class was asked to write out
the Ten Commandments, one boy put down for the
fifth, "Humor your father and your mother."

Transgressor

The way of the transgressor is hard—to find out.

Truth

Craft must have clothes, but truth loves to go naked.

—Thomas Fuller

Twenty-third Psalm

A young woman named Miss Murphy was teaching a Sunday school class the Twenty-third Psalm. As the little voices chorused out, she seemed somewhere to detect a false note.

She heard the children one by one until at last she came across one little boy who was concluding with the words, "Surely good Miss Murphy shall follow me all the days of my life."

U

United

First man: Are the members of your church united?

Second man: Yes.

First man: Praise the Lord for that.

Second man: I don't know about that—they're united because they're all frozen together!

Upholstery

Albert: I hear your brother fell into an upholstery machine.

Amanda: Yes, but he's fully recovered now.

**Zacchaeus' little-known younger brother,
Zacchias, was a tack collector.**

©2000 Jonny Hawkins

V
~~~

Vacation

1st Priest: I'm on vacation and a group asked me to speak to them. I didn't bring my clerical collar.

2nd Priest: I understand your situation: A lay date and a collar short.

Basket Paul in Damascus

©2001 Jonny Hawkins

W

Winded

Visitor: Your preacher is sure long-winded!

Member: He may be long, but he's never winded.

Wish

Rudolph: What kind of dress did Cinderella wear to the ball?

Thelma: I have no clue.

Rudolph: She wore a wish-and-wear dress.

Other Books by Bob Phillips

For more information, send a self-addressed
stamped envelope to:

Family Services
P.O. Box 9363
Fresno, California 93702

Other Books by Jonny Hawkins

*The Awesome Book
of Heavenly Humor*

*A Tackle Box
of Fishing Funnies*

Wild and Wacky Animal Jokes for Kids